SCIENCE SURPRISES™

EVERYDAY PHYSICAL SCIENCE EXPERIMENTS WITH
LIQUIDS

AMY FRENCH MERRILL

The Rosen Publishing Group's
PowerKids Press™
New York

For Mikela, who loves taking a bath

Some of the experiments in this book are designed for a child to do with an adult.

Published in 2002 by The Rosen Publishing Group, Inc.
29 East 21st Street, New York, NY 10001

First Edition

Book Design: Michael Caroleo, Michael de Guzman
Project Editor: Frances E. Ruffin

Photo Credits: p. 5 (ocean) © Ralph A. Clevenger/CORBIS; p. 5 (milk shake) © Matthew Klein/CORBIS; p 5 (beakers) © James L. Amos/CORBIS; p. 5 (dripping tap) © Robert Pickett/CORBIS; all other photos by Cindy Reiman.

Merrill, Amy French.
  Everyday physical science experiments with liquids / Amy French Merrill.— 1st ed.
    p. cm. — (Science surprises)
  Includes bibliographical references and index.
  ISBN 0-8239-5801-9 (lib. bdg.)
  1. Liquids—Experiments—Juvenile literature. [1. Liquids—Experiments. 2. Experiments.] I. Title. II. Series.
  QC145.24 .M47 2002
  530.4'2'078—dc21
                                                                                    00-013050

Manufactured in the United States of America

CONTENTS

SPLISH, SPLASH, SPLUNK!

What can be sticky, slimy, or slippery? What drips, splatters, sprays, and streams? What are not round or square, flat or tall, or any shape at all? Liquids!

People use liquids every day. You probably wash your face and brush your teeth with water. You may drink orange juice and pour syrup on your pancakes for breakfast. Gasoline powers the cars, buses, or planes in which you ride. Water, orange juice, syrup, and gasoline are all liquids.

Not all liquids are alike. Some liquids are thick, like milk shakes. Some liquids are thin, like lemonade. Liquids can feel slippery, like oil, or sticky, like honey. No matter how different they might look or feel, all liquids have one thing in common—they can be poured.

The world is full of many different types of liquids. Make a list of all the liquids that you might have used today. ▶

4

What Is a Liquid?

Scientists say that a liquid is **matter** that flows. The water in rivers flows over rocks and sand. Juice flows from a pitcher to your glass. Why do liquids flow? All matter is made up of very small particles called **molecules**. The molecules in a liquid slide past each other easily. They move around to fill whatever space they are in. This is why a liquid has no shape of its own. A liquid always takes the shape of its container. Try this **experiment**. Pour the same amount of water into three clear containers of different sizes and shapes. You might use a tall glass, a medium-size bowl, and a large

MATERIALS NEEDED:
clear containers of different sizes and shapes, water, food coloring

A liquid may fill only a few inches (cm) in a large container, but the same amount may fill a small container completely.

jar. Stir a few drops of food coloring into each container. Ask a friend to guess which of the containers holds the most water. Is your friend surprised to find out that each container has the same amount of water?

A liquid has no shape of its own. It takes on the shape of the container into which it is poured. ▶

Science in a Bathtub

   Liquids may not have a shape, but they do have **volume**. A liquid's volume is how much space the liquid takes up. The next time you take a bath, try this experiment. After you fill the tub with water, use a small amount of shaving cream to mark the level of the water. The mark shows how much space the water takes up. Once you climb into the bath, look to see where the level of the water is. The level has changed! You didn't add more water, so how can the water rise? The water rises because your body takes up space, too. The difference in the water level

MATERIALS NEEDED:
brick, rock, or other heavy object, large plastic container, water, china marker

What will happen to the water level in a bowl when you add a heavy object? ▶

equals the volume of the parts of your body in the water. Here's another way to measure volume. Pour water into a large, plastic container until it is half full. Make a mark with a china marker to show the level of water. Place a brick, rock, or other heavy object into the container. Make a second mark to show the difference in water level.

◀ *Measure the volume of water before to find out how much space it takes up in a container.*

USING LIQUIDS TO MEASURE

You aren't the first person to do a science experiment while taking a bath! About 2,000 years ago, a Greek scientist named Archimedes stepped into his bath and saw the water rise around his leg. He realized that when you place an object in a liquid, the liquid moves to make room for it. Scientists have used this idea to measure the volume of different objects. Here's how:

Find a measuring cup that is marked to measure 2 cups (473 ml). Pour 1 cup (237 ml) of water into the measuring cup. Collect different objects, such as stones, marbles, or small toys. Place one of the objects in the cup. The water

> **MATERIALS NEEDED:**
> 2-cup (473-ml) measuring cup, water, small objects, china marker, sheet of paper, pencil

level rises, just as it did when you got in the bathtub. Look at the new level of water in the cup. If the water level rose to 1 ½ cups (355 ml), then the volume of the object is ½ cup (118 ml). On a sheet of paper, measure the volume of each of the objects. Which object has the greatest volume?

Different units are used to measure solids and liquids. For example, 1 milliliter (ml) of liquid is equal to 1 cubic centimeter (cc) of a solid. ▶

A Liquid's Skin

The molecules that make up a liquid **attract** each other. This force holding the surface of a liquid together is called **surface tension**. Surface tension makes the surface of a liquid act like an **elastic** skin.

You can observe surface tension at work. Gather about 30 pennies or paper clips and a small glass. Fill the glass to the brim with water. Carefully drop the pennies or paper clips in one at a time. On a sheet of paper, keep count of how many pennies or clips you add. Watch carefully as the surface of the water rises. When the water rises just above the **brim** of the glass, it seems to be held by an invisible skin! The water doesn't spill over the side. How many pennies or clips can you drop in before the surface tension, or skin, breaks?

How strong is surface tension? Some insects use surface tension to walk on water! ▶

MATERIALS NEEDED:

small drinking glass, water, 30 pennies or paper clips, sheet of paper, pencil

The water in this glass is above the brim, but the surface tension keeps the water from flowing over the side. ▶

STRONG LIQUIDS

What happens when you spill a glass of milk? The milk becomes a stream of moving liquid. It can make a real mess! In fact, a moving liquid can be a powerful force that is able to change the **environment** in its path. Over time, the water flowing in rivers or waterfalls can wear down even solid rock. A heavy rainfall may damage sand dunes on the beach. Giant **tidal waves** can wipe out an entire town in a matter of hours.

This experiment will show you how moving liquids can create change. Use rocks and plant soil in a shallow pan to make a model of a hill. Fill a pitcher, watering can, or other container with water. Pour the water over your

MATERIALS NEEDED:
small rocks, potting soil, shallow aluminum pan, pitcher or other pouring container, water

hill. What happens? The force of the water moving over the rocks and soil changes the shape of your hill. When water moves over rocks or soil, it causes **erosion**. Erosion can change the shape of mountains.

▲

How is water pouring from your pitcher like a rainstorm?

The force of water can flatten your hill. In nature, moving water can create caves and valleys. ▶

A SALTY SOLUTION

Liquids can **dissolve** gases, other liquids, or even solid materials. When a gas, liquid, or solid is spread evenly throughout a liquid, a **solution** is formed. Chocolate milk, tomato soup, and ocean water are all examples of solutions.

You may think a material that has dissolved in a liquid has disappeared, but it hasn't. Try this experiment. In a shallow bowl, stir 2 tablespoons (30 ml) of salt into ½ cup (118 ml) of warm water. Stir the salt until you can't see it anymore. Set your saltwater solution in a warm, dry place for a few days. What

MATERIALS NEEDED:
2 tablespoons (30 ml) of salt,
½ cup (118 ml) of warm water,
a shallow bowl

16

The salt in our food is formed when salt water from the oceans and seas overflow into shallow pools and evaporate. ◀

happens to your solution? The water **evaporates**, but the salt is left behind.

Water has evaporated from this bowl. Can you think of other examples of evaporation? ▶

LOSING LIQUIDS

Did you know that liquids can change? When a liquid becomes very hot, it changes into a gas. When a liquid becomes very cold, it changes into a solid. You see water change from a liquid to a solid when you make ice cubes. If you ever have seen water boiling on the stove, you also have seen liquid water change to a gas. The bubbles in boiling water are an invisible gas we call steam.

Making ice cream is a fun way to change a liquid into a solid. Mix together cream, sugar, and vanilla in a plastic cup. Fill ⅓ of

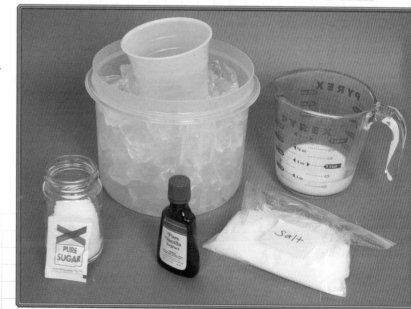

MATERIALS NEEDED:
¼ cup (59 ml) whipping cream, 2 tea-spoons (10 ml) sugar, 4 tablespoons (59 ml) salt, 1 drop vanilla extract, plastic cup, large plastic bowl, crushed ice, 2 metal spoons

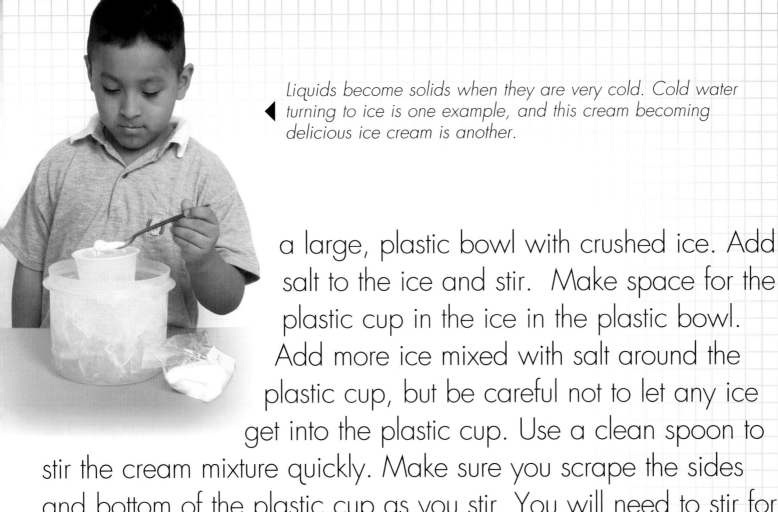

Liquids become solids when they are very cold. Cold water turning to ice is one example, and this cream becoming delicious ice cream is another.

a large, plastic bowl with crushed ice. Add salt to the ice and stir. Make space for the plastic cup in the ice in the plastic bowl. Add more ice mixed with salt around the plastic cup, but be careful not to let any ice get into the plastic cup. Use a clean spoon to stir the cream mixture quickly. Make sure you scrape the sides and bottom of the plastic cup as you stir. You will need to stir for about 20 minutes.

THE WONDER OF WATER

Which liquid is everywhere you turn? Water! People use water for bathing, drinking, and cooking. Plants need water to grow, and many plants and animals make their homes in lakes, rivers, and oceans. Water is an important means of transportation, too. Did you know that your body is almost two-thirds water? Water is in every **cell** of your body. It is part of your blood, tears, sweat, and saliva. People could not live without liquid water.

Here's an experiment to try. Use a scale to weigh a fresh carrot that has been cut

MATERIALS NEEDED:
scale, a carrot cut into several
small pieces, paper plate,
sheet of paper, pencil

Just for fun, try this experiment with other fruits or vegetables. Compare them to see which contain and lose the most liquid. ◀

into several small pieces. Record the weight of the carrot. Set out the carrot pieces on a paper plate for several days, then weigh the carrot again. Compare the new weight of the carrot to the weight you recorded earlier. What happened? The carrot weighs much less than it did before! That's because there was a lot of water in a carrot. The water evaporated when the carrot was left out in the air.

How many ounces or grams lighter does your carrot weigh after the water evaporates? ▶

ALL-PURPOSE LIQUIDS

How many liquids can you name? Milk, juice, tea, oil, and gasoline are a few liquids. Dish-washing soap, shampoo, and some paints are other liquids. Liquids are an important part of our everyday lives. We drink and eat some liquids. We rely on other liquids for fuel. Still other liquids help us keep ourselves and other things clean.

Water is a very special liquid. Plants, animals, and people need water to survive. We use water to grow the crops we need for food, and we use it to manufacture things. In the past, the water in streams and rivers was used to power waterwheels. Today water from lakes or **reservoirs** is used to provide electricity for towns and cities all over the world.

Liquids are a form of matter that matter very much!

Glossary

attract (uh-TRAKT) To cause other people, animals, or things to want to be near you.

brim (BRIM) The edge or rim of a hollow container.

cell (SEL) One of the many tiny units that make up all living things.

dissolve (dih-ZOLV) To seem to disappear when mixed with a liquid.

elastic (ih-LAS-tik) Able to go back to its own shape after being stretched.

environment (en-VY-urn-ment) The living conditions that make up a place.

erosion (ih-ROH-shun) When an object is slowly worn away.

evaporates (ih-VA-puh-rayts) Changes from a liquid to a gas.

experiment (ik-SPER-uh-ment) A test that is used to discover or prove something by watching the results.

matter (MA-tur) The material that makes up something.

molecules (MAH-lih-kyoolz) Tiny building blocks that make up a substance.

reservoirs (REH-zuhv-warz) A man-made lake where water is stored.

solution (suh-LOO-shun) A mixture of two substances, one of which dissolves in the other.

surface tension (SER-fis TEN-shun) The force that holds the surface of a liquid together.

tidal waves (TY-dul WAYVZ) Unusually high waves.

volume (VOL-yoom) How much space matter takes up.

Index

Web Sites

To learn more about liquids, check out this Web site:

http://www.chem4kids.com/matter/index.html

24